Jay Beckwith and Julia Morgan
Two Builders

by Jacqueline Maloy and Mary Beth Spann

Table of Contents

Introduction

Across California, there are many beautiful places. You can find everything from wide, sandy beaches to tall, snowy mountains. Those things are all found in nature. But people have made California beautiful, too. Many people have built amazing places around the state. Their work has helped make California a nice place to live.

⟳ Builder Jay Beckwith says play is magical and playgrounds should be, too.

Two of those builders are Jay Beckwith and Julia Morgan. Jay Beckwith designs playgrounds. Each one has unusual, interesting shapes. Julia Morgan designed some of the most beautiful and well-known buildings in the state. Both Beckwith and Morgan worked to make California a beautiful place.

↻ This is Julia Morgan when she was a student learning about building design.

Chapter 1

Meet Jay Beckwith

Is Jay Beckwith an artist, a builder, or an inventor? He would say he is all three. Beckwith creates playgrounds which many people have called works of art. Each has amazing **equipment** and structures with lots of different shapes. Children can climb on them, through them, or under them.

Beckwith grew up in California in the 1950s. When he was a boy, he didn't play in a playground. Instead, he played in trees and creeks. Young Jay was smart but did not like schoolwork. What he really loved was art. He decided to become an artist when he grew up.

This is Jay Beckwith as a young boy. ⤵

In the 1960s, people had new ideas about how kids play. They believed playgrounds should be more than places to swing or slide. They should be places to learn, too. Beckwith saw how boring most playgrounds were. He wondered if he could make them better. So, he built new kinds of playgrounds that he called **Playspaces**.

⟳ This Playspace was made out of wood instead of metal, unlike other playgrounds at the time.

Jay Beckwith used his imagination to plan each Playspace. In his mind, he pictured kids having fun. He imagined children playing all kinds of games. Some games were big and noisy. Others were small and messy. Beckwith tried to picture what equipment the kids would play on and how the whole playground would look. He tried to think of a playground that was fun, but also safe.

Beckwith kept those ideas in mind as he created a model. His model was a small version of a playground. It was a guide that helped him build the real thing.

Beckwith used a computer to make this model. ⮑

Beckwith did not build his Playspaces alone. Parents, teachers, store owners, and other people in the community helped. Some donated their time. Others contributed money. They all wanted kids to have great places to play, too.

Today, Jay Beckwith still builds big Playspaces. He also builds mini playgrounds he calls **FingerParks.** Each is small enough to fit on top of a table. Beckwith loves thinking about his work. He never knows what he will imagine next. But there is one thing he does know. His mind is his best playground!

↻ Children play with toys on one of Beckwith's FingerParks.

Chapter 2

Meet Julia Morgan

Julia Morgan was an **architect** at a time when few women worked in this field. An architect is a person who creates the plans for buildings. She lived and worked in San Francisco and was considered the city's best architect.

Morgan was born over a hundred years ago. She grew up with her family in California, a place she loved all her life.

This is Julia Morgan when she was about six years old. ⊃

When she grew older, Morgan went to college at the University of California at Berkeley. She studied **engineering**, the science of building. There were not many women students at her school.

After college, Morgan lived in France. There, she studied at a school for artists and architects. She was the first woman to study architecture at that school. Many people at that time were unaware that women could be as good at architecture as men could be. Morgan won several medals and awards for her work.

⌂ Morgan was honored for her drawing of a theater.

After she finished her training, Julia Morgan returned to California. In 1904, she started a business in San Francisco. One of her first jobs was for Mills College of Women in the nearby city of Oakland. Morgan designed a bell tower and a library for the school.

Two years later, a major earthquake struck the San Francisco area. Hundreds of buildings were destroyed. Yet Morgan's bell tower and the library designed stayed put. People realized she knew how to plan strong, **sturdy** buildings. After the earthquake, Morgan and other architects had a lot of work. There was so much to rebuild!

The 1906 San Francisco earthquake damaged many buildings. ⤴

Morgan began to design centers for the Young Women's Christian Association, or YWCA. This organization helped women who lived on their own. The YWCA offered its members housing, classes, and activities.

From her time living in France, Morgan knew what it was like to start over in a new place. She kept that in mind as she planned the YWCA centers. Her designs made life better for the women who used them. Along with housing, the buildings had pools, gyms, and classrooms.

◔ Morgan became famous when she redesigned the Fairmont Hotel in San Francisco.

11

Julia Morgan also designed churches and schools. She planned St. John's Presbyterian Church. It had wooden beams across the ceiling that served as decoration.

The schools Morgan designed were special, too. She liked to give each classroom a door that led outside.

Several women's groups also worked with Morgan. They asked her to plan buildings that would help the poor. These groups hired Morgan because they liked and respected her work. They also knew it was not easy for a woman to work as an architect. Men often did not take the work of women seriously.

Even women's clothes made the job harder. When Morgan was young, women wore long skirts. The skirts made it difficult to walk around construction areas or to climb a ladder. But Morgan came up with a solution. When she was at a building site, she still wore a long skirt. But she also wore men's pants under it!

↻ St. John's Presbyterian Church was later renamed the Julia Morgan Center for the Arts.

In 1919, Julia Morgan took on a big **client**. Millionaire William Randolph Hearst wanted to build a home in California. He decided to hire Morgan because she was his mother's favorite architect. The **estate** she designed for him included a huge house. It had gardens, swimming pools, and even a zoo! Hearst's home took 28 years to construct. It became Morgan's most famous building.

Today, many people love to see Julia Morgan's beautiful buildings. She designed amazing places that anyone can enjoy.

⌓ The beautiful home Morgan designed is now a museum known as Hearst Castle.

Glossary

architect *(AHR-ki-tekt)* a person who designs and draws plans for buildings *(page 8)*

client *(KLIGH-uhnt)* a person who hires someone else for a service *(page 14)*

engineering *(en-juh-NEER-ing)* the science or profession of putting things and energy to use, such as building new things *(page 9)*

equipment *(ee-KWIP-muhnt)* any tools, machines, or structures a person can use to do an activity, such as swings or a slide *(page 4)*

estate *(e-STAYT)* a large piece of land with a large house *(page 14)*

FingerParks *(FING-gur-pahrks)* Jay Beckwith's small playgrounds that can be placed on tables for children to use with small toys *(page 7)*

Playspaces *(PLAY-spay-sez)* Jay Beckwith's large playgrounds *(page 5)*

sturdy *(STUHR-dee)* strong, solidly built *(page 10)*

Comprehension Check

Summarize

Use a Main Idea and Details Chart to write down information about Jay Beckwith and Julia Morgan. Then use the chart to write a summary about this book.

Main Ideas	Details

Think and Compare

1. Reread page 9. What is the information on this page mainly about? Which details help you learn more about the main idea? *(Identify Main Idea and Details)*

2. What would you include in a playground if you were building one? Would you include any of Jay Beckwith's designs? *(Apply)*

3. How might Julia Morgan have changed the way women were viewed and treated during her lifetime? *(Analyze)*